Cocktails should be fun.

Cocktails should be simple.

Cocktails should be social.

shake

A NEW PERSPECTIVE ON COCKTAILS

eric prum & josh williams

CLARKSON POTTER/PUBLISHERS
NEW YORK

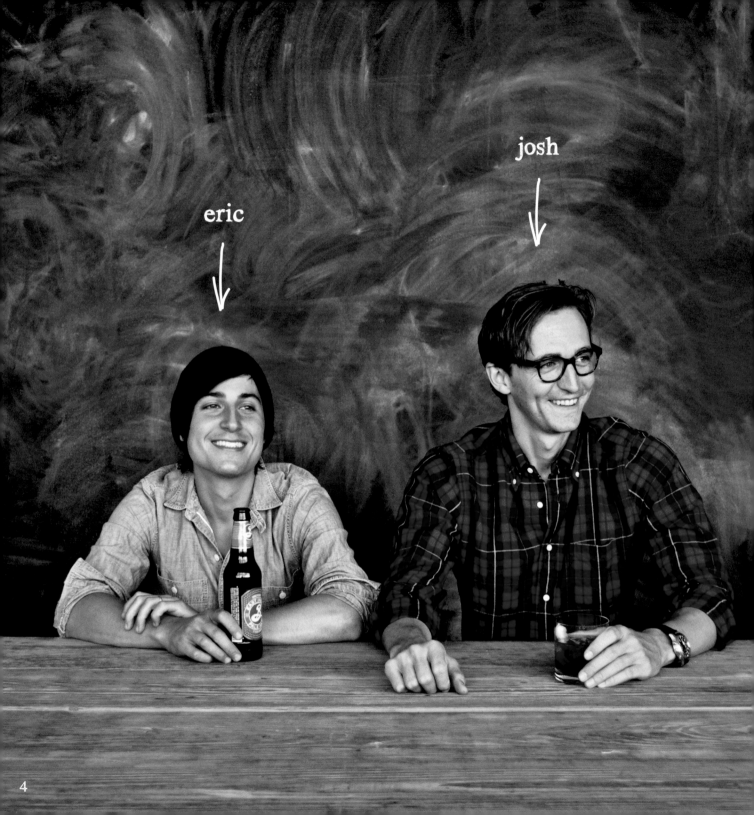

eric

josh

foreword *by* lauren sloss

Do you remember your first cocktail party? I do . . . blurrily. It centered around a worn bar somewhere upstairs in a frat house—a major upgrade from the basement. We probably dressed up, and we definitely had a good time. As for the drinks? I'd be hard-pressed to cite any options that went much beyond "vodka, and _____."

Oh, am I glad to have grown up and out of those supposed "cocktail" days. Adulthood has brought with it the joys of brown liquor, cocktail bars, and a continuous stream of professionally mixed libations that not only make for a good time, but taste damn good, too. Even better? I've gotten to write about the many delicious drinks out there for the sipping in both San Francisco and New York, two cities with full-blown cocktail obsessions. You know you've made it when you get to have a drink (or five) and call it work.

But here's the thing: often, it felt like the "good" drinks were reserved for the bars, while drinking at home with friends was still limited to frat house concoctions. It's too wide a divide, between the Jack-and-gingers of your home bar and the smoked, barrel-aged, rare batch tequila flips with housemade bacon-infused unicorn hair bitters* of the professional cocktail world. Thankfully, *Shake* is here to help fill that gap.

When I met Eric and Josh after moving to Brooklyn, I knew pretty much instantly that they were guys who spoke my language. I was then, and still am, blown away by the knowledge, enthusiasm, and passion that these two have for creating and crafting new drink concepts. Not surprisingly, ours was a friendship that was built around good drinks, good food, and plenty of laughter. The thing is, the drinks were always delicious, whether we were sitting down to dinner or pre-gaming a night out in the 'burg.

And that is exactly what *Shake* is all about: that cocktails can and should be delicious and fun, for all occasions. It's a collection of thoughtful, seasonal, and undeniably tasty cocktail recipes that are accessible enough for anyone to make. *Shake* brings the delicious cocktails of the bar home—and has a blast doing it. But you don't have to take my word for it. Grab your shaker, pick a page, and get cocktailing. The only really necessary ingredient is good friends—they'll make the good times just about inevitable.

*Sourced from cage-free unicorns that are unharmed in the plucking process.

Lauren Sloss is a regular contributor to Serious Eats and The Bold Italic

introduction

We love cocktails. We have for a long time. But recently, we looked around and realized that, while cocktail bars had sprouted up across the world, good drinks still couldn't be found in the place where we had always mixed them: at home with friends.

So we set out from our workshop in Brooklyn, New York, to come up with a solution. What resulted is one part instructional recipe book, one part photo journey through our year of cocktail crafting, and one part inspirational pep talk. We think we've ended up with something unique: a cocktail book that expresses our seasonal and straightforward approach to drinks and entertaining, and reminds us that, above all, mixing cocktails should be fun, simple, and social:

Cocktails should be fun. If they're not fun, why make them?! How do you keep them fun? Be creative. Use interesting ingredients you find at the market. Improvise on a recipe you have mastered. Take cocktails with you on the go (we have included an example of how we do this each season).

Cocktails should be simple. Your ingredient list for a cocktail should include, at maximum, five items—and try to keep your ingredients seasonal and fresh!

Cocktails should be social. Drinking alone is acceptable on some specific occasions, like after a bad breakup, or while waiting for others to drink with. But they're so much better when they're shared. Cocktails naturally bring people together. Don't believe us? Just try bringing makings for a delicious cocktail to the next house party you're attending and see what happens.

Our genuine hope is that this book inspires you to take delicious cocktails out of the bar and into your hands—and helps you do just that. So, grab some friends, turn the page, and start shaking up drinks in a whole new way.

Eric & Josh

Given my background in cooking, I'm a big believer in drinking the way that I try to eat: seasonally and creatively. I love using ingredients at their peak freshness and improvising with what I find. Farmers markets are a great source of inspiration and simple but flavorful ingredients. That being said, there's never a time of year when you won't find me drinking a solid Rye Old Fashioned (page 45).

josh

I love entertaining. There's nothing better than spending a night with good friends and great drinks. That's why I have my go-to recipes that can always be cranked out for a crowd. When it's warm out, I usually shake up the Montauk Mule (page 101), and in colder weather, I go for my personal favorite—the Rosemary Maple Bourbon Sour (page 139). I tend to stick with the cocktails I know well when hosting, so I can enjoy the party while still mixing awesome drinks.

eric

how
we
shake.

Table of

Here are the fundamentals of how we make our cocktails, from what kinds of liquor we always have on hand to the best way to shake a drink. This isn't a comprehensive A–Z of how to make cocktails, just a handful of simple, key points that will make your drinks all the more delicious.

Winter in New York can be brutal, especially for two guys from Virginia. We get through the coldest of months by mixing up stiff cocktails and celebrating the holidays with good friends. Drinks like the Sage Advice and our 'Nog are filled with the best flavors of the season, from winter sage to festive spices. Oh, and we tend to hang out in our workshop in Brooklyn and drink whiskey. Lots of whiskey.

When the weather turns cooler, our drinks turn darker and stronger. As we move  fall flavors, from Concord grapes to fresh apple cider to warm spices. And we warming happy hour drinks, obviously.

Contents

When spring arrives, so do fresher ingredients, and our cocktails are fueled by the likes of sweet blackberries, tart rhubarb, and fragrant lilac blossoms. The highlight of our spring: we're off to the races, rickeys and juleps in hand.

New York summer means sticky heat waves . . . and refreshing cocktails to counteract them. Lighter concoctions like the Hop, Skip, Go Naked and Spicy Mezcalita—along with lush plums, juicy watermelon, and cooling mint—offer relief, as do visits to the local farmers markets in full bloom and a weekend at the beach.

into sweater weather, we mix drinks with the last of summer's bounty and tradi-
we even escape the city for a long weekend on a perfect lake in Maine—complete

Cocktail Crafting 101

Cocktail Crafting 101

stock your bar

Stocking your home bar can be daunting: the sheer number of options on the market is often distracting and can paralyze the best of us. To help you out, we put together a collection of a dozen essential spirits that we love and use consistently. With these bottles, you'll be able to craft just about every recipe in this book and make something to suit to any guest's tastes.

aperol

aromatic bitters

bourbon

cointreau

gin

mezcal

while we love these brands of "spirits, don't worry if you can't find one. just ask a friend for their favorite"

rum
(dark)

rum
(light)

rye

vodka

tequila

st-germain

Every drink has a type of glassware that practically begs to go with it. The perfect glass shape can even improve the flavor of a cocktail! Who knew? Well, now we do—and we've narrowed down our go-to drink receptacles to the five easy-to-find types below. With these on your shelf, you can properly serve up any concoction you come up with (and they look pretty good, too). We're getting thirsty just looking at this.

glassware

a
collins

b
pint

c
coupe

d
rocks

e
tumbler

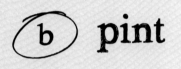 **collins**

The Collins is a classic glass that takes its name from the Tom Collins cocktail and is designed for carbonated drinks. The tall, slim shape helps effervescent cocktails stay that way long after they're poured.

SIZE: 10–14 ounces

 **pint**

The pint glass is meant for larger mixed drinks that generally have a lower alcohol content, like beer cocktails (unless you're really getting after it). On our bar, we like to substitute traditional pints for 16 ounce Mason jars.

SIZE: 16 ounces

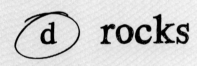 **coupe**

The coupe became popular in the 1930s as a Champagne glass, but today, it's making a well-deserved comeback in the cocktail world. Smaller than most other glasses, this one's perfect for small doses of potent cocktails served "up" (without ice).

SIZE: 4–6 ounces

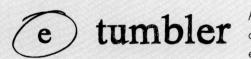 **rocks**

The rocks glass might be the most versatile glass out there. It's capable of handling just about any cocktail, and drinks served over ice ("on the rocks") usually find their way into one of these. If you only buy one type of cocktail glass, make it this one.

SIZE: 6–10 ounces

e tumbler

A tumbler is a sturdy, flat-bottomed glass with a slightly wider mouth than a rocks. We use tumblers when we're cocktail-crafting on the go, given their easy pour-ability and the way they can take a licking in transit.

SIZE: 6–10 ounces

ice

ice is a crucial component of any cocktail, and the type of ice you use when shaking and serving can dramatically affect your drink. If the ice you use melts too quickly, you'll end up with watered-down flavors; too slowly, and you could end up blowing your taste buds away with high-octane alcohol. Really, ice serves two purposes in cocktail-making. First, while shaking or stirring, it chills your cocktail and dilutes it to the perfect, drinkable strength. Then, it keeps the finished

cubes

Ice cubes are used in cocktails when you want to keep your drink cold but you don't want it to get diluted. We always try to use fresh, large cubes—between one and two inches in diameter. Using a larger cube slows the melting process by decreasing the surface area of the ice and helps you avoid having a drink that gets watered-down too fast after you pour it into a glass.

"different types of cocktails

product cool over time as you sip on it. In both instances, ice is just doing what ice does best: melting. This means that much of what ends up in your finished cocktail actually started out as ice! Now, just imagine those old, freezer-burned cubes imparting all that funky, frosty flavor into your otherwise-tasty drink. This is why we're so obsessed with the quality and shape of our ice. While you should always use cubes for shaking or stirring your cocktails, when it comes to serving, we like to break it down into two options:

(b)

crushed

Crushed
ice is usually used in strong
cocktails with high alcohol contents
that need to be diluted after they're served.
Due to its smaller size per piece, crushed ice offers
more surface area to chill a cocktail quickly, and it melts
much faster than a standard cube. And it's easy to make: all
you need is a hefty muddler and a cocktail shaker. Just fill
the shaker one-third of the way up with ice and muddle until
it's broken up into pieces that are about the size of dimes.

call for different types of ice"

Pure Cane
Sugar Cubes

sugar

Sweetness creates a balance of flavors in a drink. It naturally tames the acidity of citrus and tempers the burn of high-proof spirits. We prefer to use pure cane sugar (also called Turbinado or Demerara sugar) in our cocktails—it adds a depth of flavor that you miss out on with highly refined white sugar.

Sugar appears in our drinks in two distinct forms:

(a) cubes

There's something about muddling rough-cut sugar cubes with hand-selected, fresh ingredients that feels so satisfying. Using cubes over simple syrup can serve a purpose, too: the granules of sugar help break down other cocktail components and release extra flavor into your drink.

(b) simple syrup

Simple syrup is just that: simple. It's just equal parts sugar and water combined and heated to make syrup. We use it in cocktails that don't require muddling, and in situations when we need to make drinks for a large crowd. It takes only minutes to make and keeps in the fridge for about one month.

<u>The Recipe</u>
Makes 1.5 Cups
1 cup pure cane sugar (also called Turbinado or Demerara)
1 cup water

i. Bring the sugar and water just to a simmer over medium heat, stirring until dissolved.

ii. Remove from heat and let cool to room temperature. Store covered in the refrigerator.

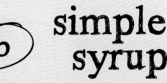

"this is what sugar with flavor looks like"

muddle

Muddling is the process of crushing ingredients in the bottom of a cocktail shaker to infuse their essence into a drink. Whether it's with a juicy strawberry, a crisp cucumber, or a mint sprig, a quick muddle can break down these ingredients and release a wealth of flavor into your cocktail.

We like to use an old-fashioned 10-inch wooden muddler to get good leverage on the ingredients (but we've been known to use a kitchen spoon in a pinch).

"we use a a flavor muddler as releaser"

shake

Shaking a cocktail properly achieves three main things: it chills the ingredients quickly; it dilutes the cocktail to a drinkable level; and, perhaps most important, it actually adds air bubbles and tiny bits of ice to the mix, which give your drink body and texture.

Every cocktail requires a certain amount of shaking, so we've simplified the process by establishing three basic categories:

short
(3 seconds)

medium
(10 seconds)

long
(15 seconds)

Winter

Winter

✕ ✕ ✕

"pink peppercorns are more floral than spicy and make for a surprising addition to this gin cocktail"

Pink Peppercorns —

The
Bushwick Spice
Trade.

We like to pair this intriguing cocktail with spicy Asian take-out when frigid temperatures call for a night in.

THE PARTICULARS
makes two drinks

4 shots gin

4 cubes cane sugar

1 shot fresh lemon juice

4 slices of fresh ginger (plus 2 for garnish)

1 teaspoon of pink peppercorns

4 basil leaves

i. Add the cane sugar cubes, lemon juice, ginger, pink peppercorns, and basil to the shaker.

ii. Muddle the ingredients in the bottom of the shaker until thoroughly crushed and the sugar has mostly dissolved.

iii. Add the gin and ice to above the level of the liquid and shake vigorously for 15 seconds.

iv. Strain the mixture into chilled coupes and garnish with remaining ginger.

What is one shot, exactly? It's technically 1.5 ounces, but as long as you maintain the right ratios, your cocktails will taste just fine.

Simple
Syrup

Grapefruit
Zest

Pink
Grapefruit

Winter
Sage

Sage
Liquor

Cava

Winter Sage

"winter sage comple-
liquor in this cold-
ments a sage-infused
weather cocktail"

The Sage Advice.

Sweet pink grapefruit and citrusy Spanish cava come together with a double-dose of sage (both the herbaceous spirit from Art in the Age of Mechanical Reproduction and a helping of the fresh, winter-proof herb) to create this cocktail.

THE PARTICULARS
makes two drinks

1 shot Sage liquor

2 shots fresh pink grapefruit juice

1/3 shot simple syrup (see page 19)

2 strips of grapefruit zest

2 sage leaves (plus 2 to garnish)

Spanish cava

i. Crush the sage leaves and grapefruit zest in your hand and add them to the shaker.

ii. Add the Sage liquor, grapefruit juice, and simple syrup to the shaker.

iii. Add ice to above the level of the liquid and shake vigorously for 3 seconds.

iv. Strain the mixture into chilled coupes and top with cava. Garnish with sage leaves.

 Don't have Sage liquor? Don't sweat it. Just substitute in your favorite gin.

Lavender

Gin

Seltzer

Lemon

St-Germain

Lavender

"drying herbs during provide you with ingredients all the summer can flavorful cocktail year round"

The L Train.

Late winter in New York City is often bitterly cold and dark—and it sometimes leaves us yearning for the summer long past. To combat those bleak spells, we turn to dried lavender that we've saved from the summer's farmers markets as a reminder that warmer weather will return.

THE PARTICULARS
makes two drinks

2 shots gin

1 shot St-Germain

1/2 shot fresh lemon juice

2 sprigs of lavender (plus 2 to garnish)

Seltzer

i. Add the gin, St-Germain, lemon juice, and lavender to the shaker.

ii. Add ice to above the level of the liquid and shake vigorously for 10 seconds.

iii. Strain the mixture into chilled coupes and top with seltzer. Garnish with remaining lavender sprigs.

Cinnamon

Vanilla
Ice Cream

Nutmeg

Bourbon

Dark Rum

"you can make a pretty damn good eggnog using high quality store-bought vanilla ice cream"

Vanilla
Ice Cream

The 'Nog.

Eggnog can be a pain to make, and most store-bought versions fall flat. But we can't go through a holiday season without some of this quintessential festive drink, so here's our version of a super quick and tasty 'nog—perfect for your next holiday gathering.

THE PARTICULARS
makes two drinks

1 shot bourbon

1 shot dark rum

2 scoops of vanilla ice cream

1/2 teaspoon of ground cinnamon

1/2 teaspoon of ground nutmeg (plus a pinch to garnish)

i. Add the bourbon, rum, ice cream, cinnamon, and nutmeg to the shaker.

ii. Shake vigorously for 10 seconds.

iii. Strain the mixture into chilled coupes and garnish with remaining nutmeg.

 Want to take this cocktail to the next level? Use freshly grated nutmeg. It's worlds better than the powdery stuff you get in plastic jars at the store.

Winter in the Workshop
Brooklyn, New York

Our workshop sits in a gritty industrial zone in Bushwick, Brooklyn. In the last few years, cheap rents (and cheaper bars) have started to attract art studios, small businesses, and other independent creators to the neighborhood. It's a dusty, dirty, magical place where you now have to be equally careful to avoid being hit by a cement truck or a hipster on a fixed-gear when you are walking to work. In our workshop we have created a space we can transform

into whatever we need it to be for recipe-creating and product-development—be it a photo studio, test bar, an amateur woodshop (don't ask), or a place to have friends for brainstorming (and tasting) sessions. In the winter, it's the perfect spot to hunker down for the afternoon with a whiskey in hand and talk through new ideas.

The Rye Old Fashioned.

THE PARTICULARS

makes two drinks

4 shots rye

2 cubes cane sugar

10 dashes of aromatic bitters

2 strips of orange zest (plus 2 to garnish)

i.

Add the cane sugar cubes and aromatic bitters to the shaker.

ii.

Muddle the ingredients in the bottom of the shaker until the sugar has mostly dissolved.

iii.

Add the rye and orange zest to the shaker.

iv.

Add ice to above the level of the liquid and stir for 10 seconds.

v.

Strain the mixture into rocks glasses containing large cubes of ice and garnish with remaining orange zest.

Lime

Pink
Grapefruit

Tequila

Cointreau

Chile Salt

Dried Chiles

Sea Salt

"we combine equal parts dried Mexican chiles and
sea salt to make a spicy rim for this margarita"

A Mid-Winter Marg.

Margaritas aren't just for the summer-time. Winter brings beautiful citrus from the Southern states, which we use to mix up this grapefruit-fueled marg.

THE PARTICULARS

makes two drinks

3 shots of tequila

1 & 1/2 shots Cointreau

1 & 1/2 shots fresh lime juice

1 & 1/2 shots fresh grapefruit juice

2 slices of fresh lime (to garnish)

Chile salt

i. Combine the tequila, Cointreau, lime juice, and grapefruit juice in the shaker.

ii. Add ice to above the level of the liquid and shake vigorously for 15 seconds.

iii. Strain the mixture into chilled rocks glasses rimmed with chile salt and containing large cubes of ice. Garnish with lime slices.

Kale

Ginger

Cane Sugar
Cubes

Lemon

Apple
Cider

Kale

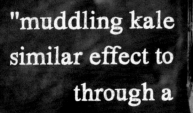

"muddling kale similar effect to through a can produce a putting the vegetable juicer"

Juicin'.

Our New Year's resolutions usually include a vow to eat and drink more healthfully . . . which is why we find ourselves whipping up this easy version of a green juice as winter comes to a close.

THE PARTICULARS
makes two drinks

8 shots apple cider

1 large handful of kale

2 shots fresh lemon juice

1 cube cane sugar

6 slices of fresh ginger

i. Add the kale, lemon juice, cane sugar cube, and ginger to the shaker.

ii. Muddle the ingredients in the bottom of the shaker until thoroughly crushed and the sugar has mostly dissolved.

iii. Add the apple cider and ice to above the level of the liquid and shake vigorously for 15 seconds.

iv. Strain the mixture into Collins glasses containing large cubes of ice.

Spring

Spring

✕ ✕ ✕

Lemon

Blackberries

Tito's Handmade VODKA

Ball MASON

100% RAW+REAL VARIETAL HONEY

SELTZER Pure

Vodka

Seltzer

Wildflower Honey

Seriously Good Seltzer

The Blackberry Fence Hopper.

The flavors of this cocktail bring us back to childhood memories of bramble scratches, sunburns, and furious neighbors yelling about us stealing berries from their yard. Minus the vodka of course . . .

THE PARTICULARS
makes two drinks

2 shots vodka

1 shot fresh lemon juice

1 shot wildflower honey

8 fresh blackberries (plus 4 for garnish)

2 slices of lemon (for garnish)

Seltzer

i. Add the lemon juice, honey, and blackberries to the shaker.

ii. Muddle the ingredients in the bottom of the shaker until thoroughly crushed.

iii. Add the vodka and ice to above the level of the liquid and shake vigorously for 10 seconds.

iv. Strain the mixture into tumblers containing large cubes of ice, top with seltzer, and garnish with remaining blackberries and lemon slices.

Celery
Leaves

Cucumber

Lime

Ginger Ale

Vodka

"celery leaves are full of flavor, and they're our pick for underrated cocktail ingredient of the year"

Celery Leaves

The Cel-Ray Spring Tonic.

Dr. Brown's celery-flavored Cel-Ray soda is our top choice to accompany an old-school deli sandwich in New York City. Here, we re-create the essence of the soda with fresh ingredients, including flavor-packed celery leaves.

THE PARTICULARS
makes two drinks

2 shots vodka

1 large sprig of celery leaves (plus 2 small sprigs to garnish)

6 slices of cucumber (plus 2 to garnish)

2 slices of lime (plus 2 to garnish)

1/2 shot fresh lime juice

Ginger ale

i. Add the celery leaves, cucumber, and lime slices to the shaker.

ii. Muddle the ingredients in the bottom of the shaker until fragrant and thoroughly crushed. Add the vodka and lime juice to the shaker.

iii. Add ice to above the level of the liquid and shake vigorously for 10 seconds.

iv. Strain mixture into Collins glasses containing large cubes of ice and top with ginger ale. Garnish with remaining celery leaves, cucumber, and lime.

Lemon

Ginger

Negra
Modelo

Mezcal

Tomr's Tonic
Syrup

"our friend Tom likes to carve ice spears with a cleaver ... not necessary for this cocktail, but still completely awesome"

Ice
Spear

The Smog Cutter.

Tom Richter, Head Bartender at The Beagle in the East Village and creator of Tomr's Tonic Syrup, came out to visit us one spring afternoon and made us this cocktail from his bar menu. We were instantly addicted to the alchemic concoction of spicy, smoky, citrusy flavors, enriched with a top-off of Negra Modelo.

THE PARTICULARS
makes two drinks

1 shot mezcal

3 slices of fresh ginger

2/3 shot Tomr's Tonic Syrup

2/3 shot simple syrup (see page 19)

2/3 shot fresh lemon juice

Negra Modelo beer

i. Add the ginger slices to the shaker and muddle until fragrant.

ii. Add the mezcal, Tomr's Tonic Syrup, simple syrup, and lemon juice to the shaker.

iii. Add ice to above the level of the liquid and shake vigorously for 10 seconds.

iv. Strain mixture into Collins glasses containing large cubes of ice and top with Negra Modelo beer.

Don't have Tomr's Tonic Syrup? No problem. Just substitute in an extra 2/3 shot of simple syrup.

Strawberries

Strawberry
Jam

Lemon

Seltzer

Vodka

Rhubarb

Strawberry
Jam

"using fruit preserves adds depth of flavor to your cocktails"

The **Strawberry Rhubarb Fizz.**

We're suckers for this classic combo of sweet strawberries and tart rhubarb: the late-spring pairing reminds us of the pies of our Southern upbringing. We like to muddle together the strawberries, rhubarb, and jam to add layers of flavors to the cocktail.

THE PARTICULARS
makes two drinks

3 shots vodka

2 tablespoons of strawberry jam

4 fresh strawberries

4 slices of fresh rhubarb (plus 2 thin spears to garnish)

1 shot fresh lemon juice

Seltzer

i. Add the strawberry jam, strawberries, rhubarb slices, and lemon juice to the shaker.

ii. Muddle the ingredients in the bottom of the shaker until thoroughly crushed.

iii. Add vodka and ice to above the level of the liquid and shake vigorously for 10 seconds.

iv. Strain mixture into Collins glasses containing large cubes of ice, top with seltzer, and garnish with spears of rhubarb.

Spring Races
Charlottesville, Virginia

Every spring, we journey down to Charlottesville, Virginia, for the (in)famous Foxfield horse races—laden with cocktail makings. Race day begins bright and early with a massive Southern brunch at Labrador Springs, a farm just outside of town. As with any good sporting event, one of the best parts of the races is the tailgate. For this one,

bow ties and sun hats are necessary, as are skeet shooting, heaping plates of food, and cocktails. Race-appropriate Mint Juleps are a classic choice, but we like to mix things up a bit and serve a Cucumber Rickey (with fresh-picked Virginia mint) alongside the more traditional race-day options.

Fresh Mint

ii. Muddle the ingredients in the bottom of the shaker until thoroughly crushed.

iii.
Add the gin and ice to above the level of the liquid and shake vigorously for 10 seconds.

iv.
Strain mixture into pint glasses containing large cubes of ice, top with ginger beer, and garnish with remaining cucumber slices and mint leaves.

THE PARTICULARS
makes two drinks

4 shots gin
1 handful of fresh mint leaves
(plus a few for garnish)
6 slices of cucumber
(plus 2 for garnish)
1 shot fresh lime juice
Ginger beer

i. Add the mint leaves, cucumber, and lime juice to the shaker.

The Cucumber Rickey.

Mint

Cane Sugar
Cubes

Lemon

Bourbon

"muddling with sugar cubes helps to break down the mint and release extra flavor"

The W&P Mint Julep.

Being from the South, we're pretty much required to have our own recipe for the perfect Mint Julep—and here it is. Juleps are traditionally served as a Kentucky Derby cocktail, but we have a habit of drinking them all spring. Try this recipe, and you'll understand why.

THE PARTICULARS
makes two drinks

4 shots bourbon

1 handful of fresh mint leaves (plus a few for garnish)

4 cubes cane sugar

1/2 shot fresh lemon juice

i. Add the mint leaves, cane sugar cubes, and lemon juice to the shaker.

ii. Muddle the ingredients in the bottom of the shaker until thoroughly crushed and the sugar has mostly dissolved.

iii. Add the bourbon and ice to above the level of the liquid and shake vigorously for 10 seconds.

iv. Strain mixture into tumblers containing crushed ice and garnish with remaining mint leaves.

Ginger

Lemon

Lilac
Blossoms

Cane Sugar
Cubes

"fresh edible flowers are a striking way to perfume a spring mocktail"

Lilac Blossoms

The Lilac Bloom.

With late spring the first farmers markets of the year arrive, and fragrant flower blossoms always make an early appearance. Here, fresh lilac blossoms perfume this spicy, aromatic, and refreshing mocktail.

THE PARTICULARS
makes two drinks

8 shots spring water

4 slices of fresh ginger

4 cubes cane sugar

1 shot fresh lemon juice

1 large bunch of spring lilac blossoms

i. Add the ginger slices, cane sugar cubes, and lemon juice to the shaker.

ii. Muddle the ingredients in the bottom of the shaker until thoroughly crushed and the sugar has mostly dissolved.

iii. Add the spring water and ice to above the level of the liquid and shake vigorously for 15 seconds.

iv. Strain mixture into Collins glasses containing layers of large cubes of ice and lilac blossoms.

Summer

Summer

✕ ✕ ✕

Cointreau

Lime

Jalapeños

Tequila

Mezcal

Fresh Jalapeños

"be sure to taste the jalapeños before using, as the spice levels can vary dangerously . . ."

The Spicy Mezcalita.

We like our margaritas spicy, smoky, and not too sweet and this "Mezcalita" delivers just that. Mezcal is made by smoking the agave plant that's usually boiled to produce tequila. That distinct smokiness combined with some jalapeño heat and just a touch of sweetness makes this Mezcalita a regular in our cocktail rotation.

THE PARTICULARS
makes two drinks

2 shots tequila

1 shot mezcal

1 & 1/2 shots Cointreau

1 & 1/2 shots fresh lime juice

2 slices of fresh jalapeño (plus 2 slices to garnish)

2 slices of fresh lime (to garnish)

i. Combine the tequila, mezcal, Cointreau, lime juice, and 2 slices of jalapeño in the shaker.

ii. Add ice to above the level of the liquid and shake vigorously for 15 seconds.

iii. Strain the mixture into chilled rocks glasses containing large cubes of ice and garnish with remaining lime and jalapeño slices.

Cane Sugar
Cubes

Summer
Ale

Lemon

Vodka

Delicious
Summer Ale

Hop, Skip, Go Naked.

We first mixed this dangerously drink-able cocktail in college . . . only back then, we used the cheapest vodka, bargain beer, and frozen lemonade concentrate, blended together in the finest of 50 gallon plastic coolers. Fortunately, we've matured (a little), and so has this brightly flavored drink: here, we make it with our favorite summer ale, quality craft vodka, and fresh-squeezed lemon juice.

THE PARTICULARS
makes two drinks

2 shots vodka

4 cubes cane sugar

2 shots fresh lemon juice

2 slices of fresh lemon (for garnish)

1 can of summer ale

i. Add the vodka, cane sugar cubes, and lemon juice to the shaker. Muddle the sugar cubes in the bottom of the shaker until the sugar has mostly dissolved.

ii. Add ice to above the level of the liquid and shake vigorously for 3 seconds.

iii. Strain the mixture into chilled pint glasses containing large cubes of ice and fill glasses with summer ale. Garnish with lemon slices.

Summer Oyster Roast
Montauk, New York

Every summer, we grab our surfboards, pack up our bags, and trade the sweltering city for the cool waves of Montauk, a formerly sleepy fishing village at the very end of Long Island. With some of the best seafood, surfing, and rugged beaches of any of the shore near New York City, "The End" has recently become a destination for city-dwellers in need of a getaway, but it still maintains its off-the-beaten-path vibe and rough edges . . . and we love it for that.

At the end of a long day on the water, nothing beats finding a quiet stretch of Ditch Plains Beach and catching one final wave before lighting up a bonfire oyster roast (the Montauk Pearl is one of the finest oysters around), complete with great friends and cold drinks.

The Montauk Mule.

i.
Add the cane sugar, lime juice, and mint to the shaker.

ii.

Muddle the ingredients in the bottom of the shaker until thoroughly crushed and the sugar has mostly dissolved.

THE PARTICULARS
makes two drinks

2 shots vodka

4 cubes cane sugar

1 shot fresh lime juice

3 sprigs of fresh mint (plus 2 to garnish)

1 bottle of Prosecco

iii. Add the vodka and ice to above the level of the liquid and shake vigorously for 10 seconds.

iv.

Strain mixture into tumblers containing large cubes of ice and fill with Prosecco. Garnish with remaining mint sprigs.

Ginger Beer

Dark Rum

Lime

Ginger

"freshly muddled ginger adds an extra spicy kick to this cocktail"

Fresh Ginger

SALT

SURFBOARDS

The Flat Ditch.

When the waves aren't cooperating, we dive into this beach-friendly cocktail, our amped-up version of a Dark and Stormy. Be sure to use a super-flavorful, high-quality dark rum for this recipe; you won't regret it.

THE PARTICULARS
makes two drinks

4 shots dark rum

1 shot fresh lime juice

6 slices of peeled fresh ginger (plus 2 to garnish)

2 slices of fresh lime (to garnish)

Ginger beer

i. Add the lime juice and ginger slices to the shaker.

ii. Muddle the ingredients in the bottom of the shaker until fragrant.

iii. Add the dark rum and shake for 10 seconds.

iv. Strain the mixture into tumblers containing large cubes of ice. Top with ginger beer and remaining ginger and lime slices.

Watermelon

Cane Sugar
Cubes

Light Rum

Fresh Watermelon

The Watermelon Daiquiri.

This daiquiri gets a seasonal kick from one of our favorite foods of the summer: sweet, juicy watermelon. We like to combine it with some all-American rum distilled just a few blocks from our workshop. What could be better for your next Fourth of July BBQ? Or, you know, any time at all. 'MURICA.

THE PARTICULARS
makes two drinks

4 shots light rum

2 cubes cane sugar

2 shots fresh lime juice

2 wedges of fresh watermelon (rind removed)

2 slices of fresh lime (for garnish)

2 slices of fresh watermelon (for garnish)

i. Add the cane sugar cubes, lime juice, and watermelon wedges to the shaker.

ii. Muddle the ingredients in the bottom of the shaker until thoroughly crushed and the sugar has mostly dissolved.

iii. Add the rum and ice to above the level of the liquid and shake vigorously for 10 seconds.

iv. Strain mixture into rocks glasses containing large cubes of ice and garnish with lime and watermelon slices.

Farmers Market Cocktails
Brooklyn, New York

We believe wholeheartedly that the idea of eating locally and seasonally should apply to cocktails just as it applies to cooking. Which is why, throughout the year, we're regulars at our local farmers markets around Brooklyn and Manhattan—and why our drinks shift with the bounty of the seasons. Spring markets bring freshly sprouted strawberries for the Strawberry Rhubarb Fizz (see page 68). Summer delivers an eye-popping array of plums for the

Summer Plum Smash (see page 114). In the fall, there are few things better than freshly pressed apple cider, which we mix into the Down Easter (see page 149). And, in the heart of winter, we turn to ingredients that we've preserved from throughout the year, like the dried New York lavender in the L Train (see page 32). It's not complicated: when you use fresh ingredients at their peak, crafting delicious cocktails comes easy.

Cane Sugar
Cubes

Summer
Plums

Plum
Liqueur

Gin

GREENHOOK
GINSMITHS

Ball
MASON

GREENHOOK
GINSMITHS

Thyme

Fresh Thyme

"fresh herbs bring aroma and layers of flavor to otherwise simple recipes—here, thyme adds a savory note to juicy plums"

The Summer Plum Smash.

Mid-July in New York means tart-on-the-outside, sweet-on-the-inside, ripe summer plums practically bursting out of their skins—how could we not put them in a cocktail? Here, we've tossed this beautiful fruit with its evil twin of an infused spirit, a Brooklyn-distilled plum liqueur, with smashing results.

THE PARTICULARS
makes two drinks

2 shots gin

2 shots plum liqueur

2 cubes cane sugar

4 small summer plums (pits removed and quartered)

4 small sprigs of fresh thyme (plus 2 to garnish)

i. Add the cane sugar cubes, plums, and thyme sprigs to the shaker.

ii. Muddle the ingredients in the bottom of the shaker until thoroughly crushed and the sugar has mostly dissolved.

iii. Add the gin, plum liqueur, and ice to above the level of the liquid and shake vigorously for 15 seconds.

iv. Strain the mixture into chilled coupes and garnish with remaining thyme sprigs.

Don't have plum liqueur? Don't sweat it. Just substitute in an extra cube of cane sugar and a half-shot of fresh lemon juice.

Strawberries   Blueberries   Raspberries

Cointreau   Rosé Wine

Fresh Summer Berries

The Frenchie.

A good muddle and a quick shake infuse French Rosé with the essential flavors of summer in this Francophile's version of a sangria.

THE PARTICULARS
makes two drinks

10 shots of French Rosé wine

2 shots of Cointreau

1 cube cane sugar

6 fresh raspberries (plus 4 for garnish)

6 fresh blueberries (plus 4 for garnish)

4 fresh strawberries (plus 2 for garnish)

i. Add the cane sugar cube, raspberries, blueberries, and strawberries to the shaker.

ii. Muddle the ingredients in the bottom of the shaker until thoroughly crushed and the sugar has mostly dissolved.

iii. Add the Rosé, Cointreau, and ice to above the level of the liquid and shake briefly for 3 seconds.

iv. Strain the mixture into tumblers containing large cubes of ice and garnish with remaining berries.

Cucumber

Lime

Spring
Water

Bush Basil

"bush basil is sweet Italian basil's spicy little cousin, just the thing for **an aromatic mocktail**"

Bush Basil

The
Bush Basil
Booster.

To make it through the heat waves that hit New York each summer we take a break from the hard stuff and hydrate with nonalcoholic mocktails, like this herbaceous combination of fresh bush basil, cucumber, and lime.

THE PARTICULARS
makes two drinks

10 shots spring water

1 shot fresh lime juice

6 small sprigs of bush basil (plus 2 for garnish)

6 slices of fresh cucumber (plus 4 for garnish)

2 slices of fresh lime (plus 2 for garnish)

i. Add the bush basil, cucumber, and lime slices to the shaker.

ii. Muddle the ingredients in the bottom of the shaker until thoroughly crushed.

iii. Add the spring water, lime juice, and ice to above the level of the liquid and shake vigorously for 10 seconds.

iv. Strain the mixture into Collins glasses containing large cubes of ice and garnish with remaining bush basil, cucumber, and lime slices.

Fall

Fall

××

Concord
Grapes

Lemon

Gin

St-Germain

Concord

Grapes

"concord grapes are the most quintessentially grapey grapes out there"

The Indian Summer.

This cocktail captures the flavors of the transition from summer to fall: Concord grapes, ripe from the hot weather, combine with St-Germain and gin for a floral kick-off to the season.

THE PARTICULARS
makes two drinks

3 shots gin

1 shot St-Germain

1 shot fresh lemon juice

8 fresh Concord grapes (plus 2 to garnish)

i. Add the Concord grapes to the shaker.

ii. Muddle the grapes in the bottom of the shaker until thoroughly crushed.

iii. Add the gin, St-Germain, lemon juice, and ice to above the level of the liquid and shake vigorously for 15 seconds.

iv. Strain the mixture into chilled coupes and garnish with remaining grapes.

Cinnamon

Milk

Simple
Syrup

Cold Brew
Coffee

Cold Brew
Coffee

"with its potent flavors, cold-brewed coffee
makes for a great cocktail ingredient"

The Mexi-Cafe.

Spice up your morning routine with this super-simple drink, which combines strong, cold-brewed coffee with sweet, woody cinnamon for an iced Mexican coffee. We wouldn't blame you if you added a little aged rum to the mix, either . . .

THE PARTICULARS
makes two drinks

6 shots strong cold-brewed coffee

2 shots whole milk

2 shots simple syrup (see page 19)

4 sticks of cinnamon (plus 4 to garnish)

i. Add the coffee, milk, simple syrup, and cinnamon to the shaker.

ii. Shake vigorously for 30 seconds. Let stand for 30 seconds.

iii. Add ice to above the level of the liquid and shake vigorously for 3 seconds.

iv. Strain the mixture into tumblers containing large cubes of ice. Garnish with remaining cinnamon.

Rosemary

Bourbon

Maple Syrup

Lemon

"dark amber maple syrup takes the place of simple syrup in this cocktail"

Maple Syrup

The Rosemary Maple Bourbon Sour.

This is, simply put, a perfect fall cocktail. So good, in fact, that we find ourselves making it over and over, all year. Dark amber maple syrup lends a deep, rich, and sweet note to this herbaceous take on a Whiskey Sour—and, yes, also qualifies it as a brunch dish.

THE PARTICULARS
makes two drinks

3 shots bourbon
1 & 1/2 shots fresh lemon juice
3/4 shot dark amber maple syrup
1 large sprig of rosemary (plus 2 small sprigs for garnish)

i. Crush the large sprig of rosemary in your hand and add it to the shaker.

ii. Add the bourbon, lemon juice, maple syrup, and ice to above the level of the liquid and shake vigorously for 15 seconds.

iii. Strain the mixture into rocks glasses containing large cubes of ice and garnish with remaining rosemary sprigs.

"caper berries stand in for olives in this twist
on a dirty martini"

Caper

Berries

The Dirty Española.

This is our take on an extra dirty Martini, given a Spanish treatment with dry fino sherry and caper berries in place of olives.

THE PARTICULARS
makes two drinks

3 shots vodka

1 & 1/2 shots caper juice

3/4 shot fino sherry

4 caper berries (for garnish)

i. Add the vodka, caper juice, and fino sherry to the shaker.

ii. Add ice to above the level of the liquid and shake vigorously for 10 seconds.

iii. Strain the mixture into coupe glasses and garnish with caper berries.

Fall on the Lake
Belfast, Maine

At the first signs of fall, we round up our friends and head north to a remote lake in the great state of Maine for a rejuvenating weekend of canoeing, fishing, and hiking. Long, leisurely days spent outdoors inevitably lead to afternoon

drinks dockside. It only takes a few rounds of local smoked fish, fresh bread, and fall cocktails for us to truly start believing the state slogan: "Maine: The way life should be."

The Down Easter.

makes two drinks

3 shots bourbon

2 shots Apple Cider Syrup (see recipe below)

1 shot fresh lemon juice

2 strips of orange zest (to garnish)

i.

Add the bourbon, apple cider syrup, and lemon juice to the shaker.

ii.

Add ice to above the level of the liquid and shake vigorously for 15 seconds.

iii.

Strain mixture into coupes and garnish with strips of orange zest.

APPLE CIDER SYRUP

makes one cup

4 cups fresh apple cider

2 strips of orange zest

Boil the apple cider and orange zest over high heat until reduced to one cup. Strain and chill before using.

149

Cinnamon

Cloves

Cane Sugar
Cubes

Orange
Zest

Aged
Rum

Aromatic
Bitters

Island

Spices

"we quick-infuse aged rum with warm island spices
for this unique old fashioned"

The Spiced Rum Old Fashioned.

The classic Old Fashioned is a simple and easily customizable cocktail base: spirit, sugar, bitters, and a garnish. That's it. For this take, we quickly infuse aged rum with fragrant island spices and orange to achieve a unique and warming cold-weather drink.

THE PARTICULARS
makes two drinks

4 shots aged rum

2 cubes cane sugar

10 dashes of aromatic bitters

2 cloves

1 stick of cinnamon (plus 2 to garnish)

2 strips of orange zest (plus 2 to garnish)

i. Add the cane sugar cubes and aromatic bitters to the shaker.

ii. Muddle the ingredients in the bottom of the shaker until the sugar has mostly dissolved.

iii. Add the aged rum, cloves, cinnamon, and orange zest to the shaker. Shake vigorously for 30 seconds. Let sit for 30 seconds.

iv. Add ice to above the level of the liquid and stir for 10 seconds.

v. Strain the mixture into rocks glasses containing large cubes of ice and garnish with remaining cinnamon and orange zest.

Dill

Pickle
Juice

Hot Sauce

Bourbon

"for those of you who don't know: a pickleback is a
shot of whiskey chased with a shot of pickle juice . . .
weird-sounding? maybe. delicious? absolutely"

Step 1   Step 2

Pickleback
Me.

Sometimes, the only remedy for a raw fall day in New York is a bracing shot, and this one's our go-to. Allegedly born in Brooklyn, the Pickleback is a concoction that combines two of our favorite things in life: bourbon and pickles. Fresh herbs and a splash of hot sauce take it up a level.

THE PARTICULARS
makes two drinks

2 shots bourbon

2 shots pickle juice

2 dashes of hot sauce

2 sprigs of fresh dill

i. Add the pickle juice, hot sauce, and dill to the shaker.

ii. Muddle the dill in the bottom of the shaker until thoroughly crushed.

iii. Add ice to above the level of the liquid and shake for 3 seconds.

iv. Pour two shots of bourbon and strain the mixture into two other shot glasses.

v. Drink the shots of bourbon followed by the shots of pickle juice.

the

end

Index
by recipe name, spirits, and key ingredients

Index

by recipe name, spirits, and key ingredients

we really need to pause and say

thank you.

Eric - To my parents, in-laws, grandparents, and siblings: Thanks so much for being untiring sounding boards for the narrative that's finally here on paper. We couldn't have done this without your support. A huge thank-you to our friends in New York—we wouldn't be here without all your help, both in the workshop and with the diligent testing of our cocktails. We promise to continue (with the fun stuff, at least)! All my gratitude to my best friend, Josh, who took a giant leap of faith to come chase our dreams at W&P. Ten years in the making, buddy—I'm looking forward to the next ten. And, to my wife, Bianca: Whether it's during a day in the workshop, a week (or five) in the warehouse, or a late night in our apartment surrounded by Mason Shakers, you've been a constant support and inspiration. Thank you. (I love you very much.)

Josh - To my mom: thank you for instilling me with the ability to truly believe any idea is possible, no matter how crazy it might sound to others. To my dad: thank you for giving me the work ethic to make some of those crazy ideas actually turn into realities. Without both of you I probably would have gotten as far as "Hm, I like cocktails," and stopped there. Thank you both for the love-filled, crazy, sometimes messy, wonderful upbringing that has made me who I am today. To my brother, sister, and all my extended family, I love you all and you can now look forward to this book for Christmas, every year for the next decade. To Eric, thanks for being the greatest business partner, idea-enabler, cocktail hand model, and best friend a guy could ever ask for. Next book we will make sure you get that manicure before we do so many knuckle close-ups. To Bianca, thank you for editing all our ramblings into what you read in this book, you are a truly talented writer. And to Rebecca: thank you for being my beautiful inspiration, my sounding board, and my tremendously patient better half. Thank you for having the courage to tell me when something I'm creating can be improved. When I get indignant it's only because I know you're right. You make me better.

Eric & Josh - To all our friends who provided hours of their time, advice, and their beautiful faces to us in return for just a few cocktails, thank you (in no particular order): Emma, Danielle, Kirby, Justin T., Justin B., Elizabeth, Jordan, Jason, The Scout, Tim, Evan, Matt, Spencer, Kieran, Sam, and JP. Lastly, a big thank you to Lauren Sloss for being the most bad-ass, whiskey drinking, dance-party-instigating, cocktail-book-foreword-writing gal we have ever had the pleasure of knowing. You all rock, drinks on us (as soon as this hangover wears off).

Eric

Josh

Our
Workshop

Copyright © 2013 by Eric Prum and Joshua Williams
All rights reserved.
Published in the United States by Clarkson Potter/Publishers, an imprint of the
Crown Publishing Group, a division of Random House, Inc. LLC, a Penguin
Random House Company, New York.
www.crownpublishing.com
www.clarksonpotter.com

CLARKSON POTTER is a trademark and POTTER with a colophon
is a registered trademark of Random House, LLC.
Originally published in the United States by W&P Design LLC, New York, in 2013.

Library of Congress Cataloging-in-Publication data is available upon request.

ISBN 978-0-8041-8673-5
eBook ISBN 978-0-8041-8682-7

Printed in China

Book and jacket design by Eric Prum and Josh Williams
Jacket photography by Eric Prum and Josh Williams

First Clarkson Potter/Publishers Edition
10 9 8 7 6 5 4 3 2

www.masonshaker.com
Follow us on Instagram, Facebook and Twitter at @masonshaker